I Wish You Were Never Born!

What Is Disability?

Penny Wordsworth

Penny Wordsworth

First paperback edition: 2023

Paperback ISBN: 9798385578627

Books Written By The Author

In Nature's Embrace
A Collection Of Poems Reflecting On My Father's Story

Jesus Of Nazareth
A Collection Of Poems Reflecting On My Father's Devotion To Jesus

Salacious
A Collection Of Poems For LGBTQ2S+ Lovers

I wish You Were Never Born!
What Is Disability?

Paradox:
Thought Experiments

A Mind And Body

A mind and body that don't comply,
Bound by chains I cannot deny,
But I am more than meets the eye,
A universe within, don't deny.

My wheelchair is not a prison,
I am not a lesser citizen,
My will to live is still driven,
My worth cannot be written.

The world may see my disability,
But my spirit is my ability,
I won't let their doubts cripple me,
My strength shines, just wait and see.

My heart beats with passion and fire,
My soul sings with a fierce desire,
My dreams will not expire,
I will rise, I won't retire.

My disability may limit me,
But I am not a tragedy,
My life has value, you can see,
I am more than just a disability.

After watching me struggle for a while, an elderly woman recently walked up to me and asked, "Have you ever said, *I wish you were never born?*"

So Vast And Wide

In this world so vast and wide,
There are those who struggle and strive,
Whose bodies and minds differ from the norm,
Whose challenges are not always easy to perform.

Some wonder why God would create,
Disability in those who cannot relate,
To a world that often judges and shames,
And forgets that we are all simply human beings with names.

But perhaps God had a greater plan,
A purpose for each unique woman and man,
To teach us all lessons about love and compassion,
To break down barriers and build bridges of inclusion.

For in the face of adversity and hardship,
We learn to appreciate the value of relationships,
To see the beauty in the differences we all sing,
To embrace diversity and the gifts it can bring.

So let us not question why God created disability,
But instead, see the opportunities for growth and humility,
And work towards creating a world that truly embraces,
All individuals, regardless of their abilities or races.

It was the first time anyone had ever asked me this question: "Have you ever said, *I wish you were never born?*"

It was the first time I had ever contemplated the question because I was too busy raising my disabled child. I was shocked and taken aback for a moment.

She went on to further comment, "I can only imagine what you go through. It must be so difficult for you or anyone else to care for a disabled child. How do you do it? Where do you find the strength to carry on?"

These were rather personal questions being asked by a complete stranger. I was not sure how to respond. I was not sure I wanted to respond.

She Carries A Weight

She carries a weight, unseen by many eyes,
A child within, a precious little life.
With each step, she wonders what has been done,
What fate will deal, what joys and pains will come.

For she knows this child, growing in her womb,
Will face a world that may not understand.
A world that sees only differences,
And judges without knowing, without a chance.

But she knows this child, she loves this child,
With a love that goes beyond all boundaries.
For she sees the beauty in the imperfections,
And knows that this child will change lives.

She wonders about the future, what it may hold,
What challenges they'll face, what obstacles unfold.
But she knows that they'll face them, side by side,
And that their love will conquer all in stride.

For this child is a gift, a blessing from above,
A miracle in every sense of the word.
And she knows that they'll face each day anew,
With courage, grace, and love that never fades.

So she carries on, with hope in her heart,
And a strength that comes from deep within.
For she knows that this child will change the world,
And that together, they'll face whatever comes, with a grin.

Before I could respond, she went on to tell me this story:

"Once upon a time, there was a young couple named Rachel and Adam. They had been together since high school and were deeply in love. They had always dreamed of starting a family, but their world was about to turn upside down.

At their 20-week ultrasound, the doctor delivered the devastating news that their baby would be born with a severe disability. The doctor urged them to consider terminating the pregnancy, but Rachel and Adam were not ready to give up on their child. They had always talked about how they would face any challenge together, and this was no exception.

The couple had a difficult conversation about what their lives would be like with a disabled child. They knew it would be a tough road ahead, with many obstacles to overcome. However, they also knew that they would love their child more than anything and were willing to do whatever it takes to give them the best life possible.

Despite their decision to continue with the pregnancy, the news was hard on Adam. He couldn't handle the thought of raising a disabled child and eventually decided to abandon Rachel, leaving her to face the challenges of pregnancy and motherhood alone.

Rachel was heartbroken, but she knew that she had to be strong for her child. She leaned on her faith and asked God to help guide her through this difficult journey.

As the pregnancy progressed, Rachel's family also began to distance themselves from her. They didn't understand why she was choosing to have a disabled child and didn't want to be a part of her life anymore.

The pregnancy was difficult, with many complications along the way. Rachel had to have several surgeries and was in and out of the hospital. But through it all, she remained strong and continued to pray for her child.

Finally, the day came for Rachel to give birth. It was a long and painful process, but Rachel remained hopeful that everything would turn out okay. However, when the baby was born, there were complications, and despite the doctor's best efforts, the baby didn't survive.

Rachel was devastated. She had gone through so much to bring this child into the world, only to have them taken away so soon. She spent the rest of her life trying to understand what had happened and why it had to happen to her.

Despite the pain and sadness that she felt, Rachel never regretted her decision to have the baby. She knew that even though their time together was brief, the love she had for her child would last a lifetime."

A Mother's Love

A mother's love is fierce and strong,
A bond that lasts forever long,
For when a child comes to this earth,
A mother's love provides them worth.

And though a child may face some strife,
A mother's love will bring them life,
Through every trial, every test,
A mother's love will give them rest.

For when a child is born disabled,
A mother's love will be enabled,
To see beyond the outward form,
And cherish every breath, every morn.

A mother's love will never tire,
In loving and caring for her child,
She'll fight for them with all her might,
To make sure they're seen in a new light.

She'll carry them through every day,
And find joy in every way,
She'll see the beauty in their smile,
And love them every single mile.

For a mother's love is like a shield,
That protects her child, making them yield,
To the world's harsh and cruel ways,
And find love and comfort every day.

So let us honor every mother's love,
For it's a gift from God above,
And celebrate every child's worth,
For they are a miracle on this earth.

While she was not explicit, I knew that she was telling me her own personal story. While, at first, I was disgusted by her comments, I understood where she was coming from. Abruptly, she departed with a solemn look on her face. It was then that I began to contemplate some of the larger questions.

In The Eyes Of A Mother
Part 1

In the eyes of a mother,
A disabled child is not a burden,
But a blessing, a unique treasure,
A true gift to humanity.

She sees beyond the limitations,
Beyond the struggles and the pain,
To a world full of potential,
Where her child can shine and reign.

She dreams of a future bright,
Full of hope and endless possibility,
Where her child can conquer all,
And live life with great ability.

She knows that strength is not measured,
By physical might or mental prowess,
But by the courage to face each day,
With a heart full of love and kindness.

Test yourself with these true or false questions:
Answers appear on the next page.

1. People with disabilities are unable to live fulfilling and happy lives.
2. Disability is only visible and physical.
3. The majority of people with disabilities require constant care and support.
4. Disabled people cannot participate in sports or physical activities.
5. The disability community is a monolithic group with shared experiences and beliefs.
6. Accessibility accommodations are only necessary for people with physical disabilities.
7. People with disabilities are less intelligent or less capable than non-disabled people.
8. Disability is always a personal tragedy that should be pitied.
9. Disabled people always want to be cured of their disability.
10. The disability community is a marginalized and underrepresented group in society.
11. People with disabilities cannot work or contribute to society.
12. Disability is a result of karma or divine punishment.
13. People with disabilities are always inspirational and courageous.
14. Disability is rare and affects only a small portion of the population.
15. Disability is caused by poor parenting or bad genes.

Answers:

1. F
2. F
3. F
4. F
5. F
6. F
7. F
8. F
9. F
10. T
11. F
12. F
13. F
14. F
15. F

What Is Disability?

Disability is not a label or a curse,
It's not a limit, it's not a shame.
It's simply a state that we traverse,
A journey that we navigate, without blame.

Disability is not a weakness or a flaw,
It's not a burden, it's not a stain.
It's simply a condition that we saw,
A difference that we learn to sustain.

Disability is not a barrier or a wall,
It's not a hindrance, it's not a defeat.
It's simply an obstacle that we call,
A challenge that we face, with our own beat.

Disability is not a sentence or a fate,
It's not a judgment, it's not a decree.
It's simply a trait that we celebrate,
A diversity that we embrace, with glee.

Disability is not a label or a curse,
It's simply a part of who we are.
It's a journey that we embrace and traverse,
A difference that we celebrate, near or far.

The World Health Organization's (WHO) International Classification of Functioning, Disability and Health (ICF) provides a widely accepted framework for understanding disability.

According to the ICF, disability is defined as "an umbrella term for impairments, activity limitations and participation restrictions," and it recognizes that disability is not just a medical issue, but also a social and environmental one. The ICF emphasizes that disability results from the interaction between a person's health condition(s) and the environmental and personal factors that can either facilitate or hinder their full participation in society.

This definition of disability emphasizes that disabilities are not solely caused by individual impairments or conditions, but also by the barriers that exist in society, such as inaccessible buildings, discriminatory attitudes, or lack of accommodations. This definition also recognizes the importance of including the perspectives and experiences of people with disabilities in understanding disability, as they are the ones who live with the effects of disability on a daily basis.

Run And Play

She watches as the other kids run and play,
Wishing she could join in and have her own way.
But her body won't let her move the same,
And her wheelchair seems to only bring her shame.

She dreams of running through the grass,
And playing tag with her friends at last.
But her legs won't obey her wishes,
And her heart aches with each missed opportunity, many misses.

She wonders why she was born this way,
And why her body won't let her have her say.
But deep inside she knows that she's not alone,
And that her spirit and strength have yet to be fully shown.

She may not walk like the others do,
But her heart and mind are just as true.
And she knows that she's capable of so much,
If only the world would see her as such.

So she keeps dreaming and hoping and praying,
For a world that's more inclusive and saying:
"I may not walk, but I can still soar,
And I will shine, with each struggle and more."

A disability can be defined as any physical, mental, cognitive or developmental condition that impairs an individual's ability to perform daily activities or limits their participation in social and economic life. Disabilities can vary in severity and impact, and can be acquired at birth or later in life due to illness, injury or environmental factors.

Examples of disabilities can include but are not limited to:

Physical disabilities such as paralysis, amputation, blindness, and deafness.

Cognitive disabilities such as intellectual disability, memory impairment, and learning disabilities.

Mental health disabilities such as depression, anxiety, bipolar disorder, and schizophrenia.

Chronic health conditions such as diabetes, cancer, and HIV/AIDS.

It's important to note that disabilities are not always visible or apparent and can vary greatly in their impact on an individual's daily life. Additionally, a disability may not define an individual entirely, and people with disabilities can still have unique strengths and abilities.

A Never-Ending Battle

The struggles of disabled people are real,
A never-ending battle, an ongoing ordeal.
We face obstacles and barriers every day,
And our efforts are often met with dismay.

Our bodies may be different, but our spirits are strong,
And we fight for our rights, for where we belong.
We push through pain and limitations, never giving in,
And we refuse to let our struggles be our final win.

We're judged by our appearance, by our lack of ability,
And we're often overlooked for opportunities, no possibility.
We're forced to navigate a world that's not always accessible,
And we're expected to be grateful, never too objectionable.

But our struggles are valid, they're a part of who we are,
And we deserve to be seen, to shine like a star.
For we are not defined by our disabilities,
But by our unique talents and capabilities.

We need more support, more understanding and care,
And we need a society that's willing to be fair.
For the struggles of disabled people are real,
But with love and acceptance, we can heal.

Let's work together to break down the barriers,
And to create a world that's fairer and freer.
For the struggles of disabled people may be tough,
But with compassion and empathy, we can rise above.

Anyone with a physical, mental, cognitive or developmental condition that impairs their ability to perform daily activities or limits their participation in social and economic life is considered disabled. This can include people with visible and invisible disabilities, and the severity and impact of the disability can vary greatly from person to person.

It's important to note that disability is a complex and diverse experience, and individuals with disabilities may have different needs, abilities, and preferences. The concept of disability also involves the interaction between the individual and the environment, including physical, social, and cultural barriers that may hinder their participation in society.

In many countries, including the United States, the definition of disability is enshrined in law. For example, the Americans with Disabilities Act (ADA) defines disability as a physical or mental impairment that substantially limits one or more major life activities, a history of such an impairment, or being regarded as having such an impairment. Other countries may have different legal definitions or none at all, but the general concept of disability remains the same.

How many disabled people are there in the world today?

It is difficult to estimate the exact number of disabled people in the world due to differences in the definitions and measurements of disability across countries and cultures. However, according to the World Health Organization (WHO), over 1.6 billion people or about 20% of the world's population have some form of disability. In other words, if **Disability** was a country, it would have the most people of any country on the Earth. More realistically, more than 75% of all people will experience some form of disability at some point in their life. The vast majority of disabilities are never counted or reported.

It's important to note that disabilities are not evenly distributed across populations, and certain groups such as women, children, and older adults are more likely to experience disability. Additionally, disabilities can be influenced by a variety of factors including socioeconomic status, geography, and environmental conditions.

The United Nations (UN) has identified disability as an important issue and has included it in the Sustainable Development Goals (SDGs), a global plan to address poverty, inequality, and environmental sustainability by 2030. The SDGs call for the inclusion and empowerment of people with disabilities and for the removal of barriers that prevent their full participation in society.

All Are Welcome

In this world we call our own,
All are welcome, all are known.
From every corner of the earth,
We celebrate each person's worth.

Diversity is our strength,
Our differences are no length.
For every person, big or small,
We create a world that welcomes all.

We open doors for those who need,
A helping hand to take the lead.
And for those who can't walk or see,
We make sure their journey's free.

We build our world with love and care,
And show the world that we are rare.
A place where everyone is free,
To live their lives happily.

We see beyond each person's shell,
And know that everyone can excel.
For in our world, we believe,
That every person can achieve.

So come and join us, one and all,
We'll build a world that stands tall.
And though our paths may differ so,
We'll make a world where everyone can go.

How has our definition of disability changed over time?

The definition of disability has evolved over time and has been influenced by various social, political, and cultural factors. In the past, disability was often viewed as a personal or medical problem that required a cure or treatment to fix. However, as society has become more aware of the social barriers that people with disabilities face, the definition of disability has shifted to a more social model.

Here is a brief overview of how our definition of disability has changed over time:

Medical Model (pre-1960s): The medical model views disability as a personal or medical problem that requires a cure or treatment. People with disabilities were often seen as abnormal or inferior, and their differences were medicalized and pathologized.

Rehabilitation Model (1960s-1970s): The rehabilitation model emphasized the need for people with disabilities to be rehabilitated and trained to become more self-sufficient. This approach focused on physical and occupational therapy and other interventions to help people with disabilities become more independent.

Social Model (1970s-1980s): The social model of disability emerged as a response to the limitations of the medical and rehabilitation models. This model views disability as a social construct rather than an individual problem. It recognizes that people with disabilities are disabled by social barriers, such as discrimination, lack of access to education, employment, and services.

Disability Rights Model (1980s-present): The disability rights model builds on the social model and emphasizes the need for equal rights and full inclusion of people with disabilities in all aspects of society. This model recognizes disability as a human rights issue and promotes the principles of accessibility, independence, and self-determination.

In recent years, there has been a shift towards the concept of neurodiversity, which recognizes that neurological differences, such as autism and ADHD, are natural variations of the human brain rather than disorders that need to be cured. This approach aims to celebrate and embrace neurological diversity and promote inclusivity for all people, regardless of their neurological differences.

From Ancient Times

From ancient times to modern days,
Disabled people suffered in many ways.
Excluded, neglected, and cast aside,
Their struggles and pain, we can't deny.

Throughout history, they faced oppression,
Discrimination, and cruel suppression.
Their bodies and minds, were deemed as flawed,
Their dignity and worth were often ignored.

They were labeled as "mad," "feeble," or "weak,"
Their rights were trampled, their futures bleak.
Their stories are countless, their pain immense,
Their voices silenced, their spirit intense.

From the asylums to the institutions,
Their lives were filled with great confusion.
Locked away from the world they knew,
Their hearts cried out for a chance anew.

But through their pain, they found their voice,
Their strength and spirit, they did rejoice.
They fought for rights, for dignity and care,
Their courage and passion, beyond compare.

Today we honor their struggles and plight,
Their voices echo in the fight for what's right.
We stand with them, in solidarity and grace,
Their journey and pain, we will not erase.

For they are the heroes, the champions of change,
Their legacy forever will remain.
Their story inspires us, to fight and unite,
To create a world where every life is bright.

What Constitutes A Disability?

The history of disability around the world is a complex and varied one, with different cultures and societies viewing disability in different ways throughout history.

In many ancient civilizations, people with disabilities were often seen as having spiritual or magical powers, and were revered and respected for their perceived abilities. For example, in ancient Greece, people with disabilities were often seen as possessing divine gifts and were even worshiped as gods. Similarly, in many Native American tribes, people with disabilities were believed to have unique connections to the spiritual world and were valued members of their communities.

However, as societies became more industrialized and urbanized, people with disabilities were often viewed as a burden on society and were marginalized and excluded from many aspects of daily life. This was particularly true during the eugenics movement of the early 20th century, which sought to eliminate people with disabilities through forced sterilization and other forms of discrimination.

Despite this history of discrimination, people with disabilities have also been at the forefront of many civil rights movements around the world. In the United States, for example, disability activists were instrumental in the passage of the Americans with Disabilities Act in 1990, which prohibited discrimination against people with disabilities in employment, transportation, public accommodations, and other areas of daily life.

Today, there is a growing recognition of the diversity and complexity of disability around the world, and a growing movement towards greater inclusion and acceptance of people with disabilities. However, much work remains to be done to ensure that people with disabilities have access to the same rights and opportunities as everyone else, and to overcome the historical legacy of discrimination and marginalization.

Their Lives Deemed Lesser

Disabled people throughout history,
Their stories oftentimes a mystery,
Their lives deemed lesser, their voices unheard,
Their worth and value consistently blurred.

Yet they have been present since the dawn of time,
Facing discrimination and stigma, a constant climb,
In ancient Greece, some were seen as divine,
But in other cultures, they were left behind.

In medieval Europe, some were revered,
But others were burned or drowned, their fate feared,
During the Renaissance, some were celebrated,
While others were locked away, their lives segregated.

In the 19th century, asylums were built,
Horrors within, their walls could never be filled,
But then came the disability rights movement,
Disrupting the status quo, a new improvement.

Disabled people demanded access and inclusion,
Breaking down barriers, creating a new fusion,
Their voices finally heard, their worth acknowledged,
A new era of acceptance finally acknowledged.

Today, disabled people continue to thrive,
Breaking barriers, pushing themselves to strive,
Their worth and value finally recognized,
A new world of inclusion finally realized.

Disabled people throughout history,
Their struggles and triumphs now part of our story,
Their resilience and strength an inspiration,
A new world of acceptance, our new foundation.

Disability Throughout History

In ancient Rome, people with disabilities were often used as performers in gladiatorial games, where they were pitted against each other or against animals for the entertainment of the crowds.

In the Middle Ages, people with disabilities were often seen as being possessed by demons, and were subjected to exorcisms and other forms of religious persecution.

During the eugenics movement of the early 20th century, people with disabilities were forcibly sterilized and institutionalized in many countries around the world, including the United States, Canada, and Germany.

In Nazi Germany, people with disabilities were targeted for extermination as part of the Holocaust, with an estimated 200,000 people with disabilities killed in gas chambers and other forms of mass murder.

The Supposed Science

Eugenics, the supposed science of better breeding,
A dark history that's often overlooked and unheeding,
A theory that sought to improve the human race,
But its practices had a terrible and unjust face.

Disabled people were often the targets of eugenicists,
For they were deemed unworthy and a drain on resources,
They were viewed as burdens to society, unfit to live,
And so, they were sterilized or left to die in the streets.

Their lives were treated as expendable, mere statistics,
Their rights and dignity were denied, their voices silenced,
Their bodies were seen as imperfect, in need of correction,
And so, they were subjected to cruel and inhumane selection.

Eugenics aimed to create a world of perfection,
A world free from flaws and imperfections,
But its vision was narrow and deeply flawed,
For it failed to recognize the beauty and worth of diversity.

Disabled people, too, have a place in this world,
Their lives are valuable, their stories should be told,
Their struggles and triumphs, their joys and sorrows,
Are all part of the tapestry of human experience, to borrow.

Test yourself with these true or false questions:
Answers appear on the next page.

1. Disability always causes pain and suffering.
2. People with disabilities are more likely to be victims of crime.
3. Disability is always visible and obvious to others.
4. People with disabilities cannot have romantic relationships or families.
5. People with disabilities should be pitied and given charity.
6. The term "special needs" is an appropriate way to refer to people with disabilities.
7. People with disabilities are always nonverbal or have speech difficulties.
8. People with disabilities cannot be leaders or decision makers.
9. Accommodations for people with disabilities are expensive and impractical.
10. Disability is a personal problem and not a societal issue.
11. People with disabilities are more likely to be unemployed or underemployed.
12. People with disabilities cannot live independently or take care of themselves.
13. Disability is caused by laziness or lack of motivation.
14. Disability is a tragedy that should be avoided at all costs.
15. People with disabilities are always happy and content with their lives.

Answers:
1. F
2. T
3. F
3. F
5. F
6. F
7. F
8. F
9. F
10. F
11. T
12. F
13. F
14. F
15. F

Euthanasia

Euthanasia is the act of intentionally ending a person's life in order to relieve their suffering from an incurable or unbearable medical condition. It is also referred to as assisted suicide or mercy killing.

There are a few countries where euthanasia is legal or decriminalized, including Belgium, Canada, Colombia, Luxembourg, the Netherlands, and Switzerland. In some states in the United States and Australia, physician-assisted dying is also allowed in certain circumstances.

Euthanasia is a highly controversial issue for several reasons. Some argue that it goes against the sanctity of life and that it could lead to the abuse of vulnerable people, including those who are elderly, disabled, or mentally ill. Others believe that individuals should have the right to decide when and how they want to end their lives, especially if they are facing unbearable suffering.

The ethical and legal issues surrounding euthanasia are complex and often deeply personal, and opinions on the matter can vary widely among individuals, healthcare professionals, and policymakers.

Disability: Barriers and Right

In many developing countries, people with disabilities continue to face significant barriers to accessing education, healthcare, and employment, and are often excluded from full participation in society.

In the United States, the 1960s and 1970s saw the rise of the disability rights movement, with activists organizing protests and demonstrations to demand greater rights and recognition for people with disabilities.

In 1993, the United Nations General Assembly adopted the Standard Rules on the Equalization of Opportunities for Persons with Disabilities, which set out a framework for promoting the rights and inclusion of people with disabilities around the world.

The Eugenics Movement: In the early 20th century, the eugenics movement gained popularity in many countries, including the United States, Canada, and Germany. Eugenicists believed that certain groups of people, including those with disabilities, were genetically inferior and should not reproduce. This led to forced sterilization laws and other forms of discrimination against people with disabilities.

The Holocaust: During World War II, the Nazi regime systematically murdered an estimated 250,000 to 500,000 people with disabilities, as well as many others deemed "undesirable" by the regime. This included people with physical and intellectual disabilities, as well as those with mental illnesses.

Disability Does Not Define Us

Disability does not define us,
Nor does it diminish our worth.
We are more than our limitations,
And we have value from our birth.

We may walk a different path,
And face challenges others don't see.
But we have strength and resilience,
And we strive for equality.

Our bodies and minds may vary,
But our humanity remains the same.
We seek love, joy, and connection,
And we deserve respect and acclaim.

So let us not be defined by labels,
But rather by our hopes and dreams.
For disabled people have much to offer,
And can change the world, it seems.

With creativity, innovation, and heart,
We can overcome any obstacle in our way.
For disability is just a small part,
Of the unique and amazing individuals we portray.

Institutionalization: For much of the 20th century, people with disabilities were often institutionalized in large, impersonal institutions. These institutions were often overcrowded and understaffed, and residents were subjected to abuse and neglect. Many people lived in institutions for their entire lives, without any opportunities for education, work, or social interaction.

Deinstitutionalization: In the latter half of the 20th century, there was a movement to deinstitutionalize people with disabilities and provide them with community-based services and supports. While deinstitutionalization has led to greater independence and integration for many people with disabilities, it has also led to challenges in providing adequate funding and services in the community.

Forced institutionalization of Indigenous people with disabilities: In many countries, including Australia and Canada, Indigenous people with disabilities were forcibly removed from their families and communities and placed in institutions. This was part of a larger policy of assimilation and colonization, and had devastating impacts on Indigenous peoples' cultures and ways of life.

In A World Of Heroes

In a world of heroes, she stands out,
A disabled superhero, with no doubt.
She may not look like the rest,
But her abilities put them to the test.

With a mind that's sharp as a knife,
And a spirit that's strong enough to fight,
She uses her disability as an advantage,
And never lets it hold her back or damage.

She may have a missing limb or a broken spine,
But her heart is full of courage and shine.
She rises up to any challenge,
And uses her unique skills to balance.

Her superpower is her perseverance,
And her determination to never surrender.
For she knows that every obstacle can be conquered,
And every battle can be won, never hindered.

She may not be the typical hero,
But she inspires others to push beyond zero.
For a disabled superhero shows us all,
With the right attitude, we can stand tall.

So let's embrace diversity and inclusion,
And see the strength in our differences, no illusion.
For a disabled superhero is proof that anything's possible,
And that we can all be heroes, unstoppable.

Deaf oppression and cultural genocide: In many societies, deaf people have been oppressed and marginalized due to their differences in communication and language. This has led to the suppression of sign languages, and attempts to "cure" or "fix" deafness through medical interventions.

Forced sterilization and abortion of women with disabilities: Women with disabilities have historically been subjected to forced sterilization and abortion, based on the belief that they should not reproduce due to their perceived inferiority or inability to care for children.

Inaccessible built environment and transportation: Many cities and public spaces around the world remain inaccessible to people with disabilities, making it difficult or impossible for them to access employment, education, and other opportunities.

She Watches From Afar

She watches from afar, with longing in her eyes,
As the other kids run and laugh; chase each other's lies.
She sits on the sidelines, in her wheelchair, all alone,
Watching them play tag, with each other they've grown.

She imagines what it's like to run free,
To feel the wind in her hair, to be just like a bee.
But her body won't let her, it's not built that way,
And her heart sinks, as she watches them play.

She wants to join in, to be a part of the fun,
But her chair feels like a barrier, in the long run.
She wishes she could run and chase and play,
But her legs won't let her, no matter how much she prays.

She tries not to let it get her down,
To focus on the good, and to turn her frown around.
For she knows that she's strong, and capable too,
And she won't let her disability define her, that's true.

So she watches and dreams, and cheers them on,
And she knows that someday, she'll find her own song.
For a disability can't hold her back forever,
And she'll find her own way, she'll never say never.

Psychiatric institutionalization and human rights violations: People with mental illnesses have often been subjected to involuntary psychiatric institutionalization, which can lead to abuses of human rights and lack of access to adequate treatment and support. This has been a particular issue in many developing countries, where mental health services are limited and underfunded.

The use of "ugly laws" in the United States, which criminalized people with visible disabilities and made it illegal for them to appear in public.

The use of electroconvulsive therapy (ECT) and other controversial treatments for people with mental illnesses, which were often administered without informed consent or proper medical oversight.

The use of lobotomy, a surgical procedure that severs connections in the brain, as a treatment for mental illness and other conditions.

Worlds Apart

Disabled and able-bodied, we may seem worlds apart,
But in truth, we share a common heart.
For we are all human, with hopes and fears,
And dreams that we hold dear.

We may move in different ways, with varied paces,
But we all seek to find our places.
For we all long for love, acceptance, and connection,
And seek to find our own unique direction.

We may face different obstacles in our paths,
But we all have the strength to overcome the wrath.
For we are all warriors, with scars and battle cries,
And we rise again, even in the darkest skies.

We may see the world through different eyes,
But we all long for peace, and the sun in our skies.
For we are all united in our humanity,
And strive to find love and community.

So let us embrace our differences and similarities,
And build a world of love, compassion, and camaraderie.
For we are all part of the same tapestry,
Disabled and able-bodied, united in our humanity.

The forced sterilization of people with intellectual disabilities in countries such as Sweden and Japan.

The use of leprosy colonies to isolate and quarantine people with leprosy (now known as Hansen's disease), which led to social stigma and discrimination against people with the condition.

The institutionalization of children with disabilities in orphanages, which often led to neglect and abuse.

The use of physical restraints and seclusion in mental health facilities, which have been linked to injuries and deaths.

Each Day

I wake up each day with a challenge,
But I don't let it define who I am.
For I am more than my disability,
And I have a purpose, a plan.

Some days the pain is overwhelming,
And the world seems to stare and judge.
But I hold my head up high,
And I won't let them push me off the ledge.

I may move a little slower,
And need some extra help along the way.
But I still have dreams to chase,
And I won't let anyone stand in my way.

I have learned to be resilient,
To face adversity with a smile.
For I know that every obstacle,
Is just another opportunity to go the extra mile.
I am a disabled person, yes,
But that's not all that I am.
For I have passions, skills, and talents,
And I won't let anything dim their flame.

So let me be me, with all my quirks,
And see me for the person I am.
For being disabled is just a part of me,
And I have so much more to give, to be, to stand.

We need support and understanding,
And for society to be more accommodating.
For the struggles of disabled people are real,
But with compassion and empathy, we can heal.

Let's work together to break down the barriers,
And to create a world that's fairer and freer.
For the struggles of disabled people may be tough,
But with love and acceptance, we can rise above.

The use of aversive conditioning techniques, such as shock therapy and behavior modification, to control the behavior of people with intellectual disabilities.

The use of animal testing to develop medical treatments and devices for people with disabilities, which has been criticized for its ethical implications.

The exclusion of people with disabilities from the military, which has been used to justify discrimination and lack of access to benefits and resources.

The use of forced medication and other coercive measures in psychiatric hospitals, which have been linked to human rights abuses and mistreatment of patients.

The lack of accessibility in educational institutions, which has limited the opportunities of students with disabilities to pursue higher education and career goals.

The use of "pity" and "inspiration" narratives in media and popular culture to portray people with disabilities, which can perpetuate harmful stereotypes and misconceptions.

The use of segregated and specialized schools for children with disabilities, which can lead to social isolation and lack of access to mainstream education and opportunities.

The lack of accessibility in public transportation, which can limit the mobility and independence of people with disabilities.

A Battle To Fight

We wake up each day with a battle to fight,
The struggles of disability, an ongoing plight.
We face barriers and obstacles at every turn,
And our efforts are often met with a stubborn concern.

Our bodies and minds may not be typical,
And our differences can make others skeptical.
We're judged by our appearances and limitations,
And often overlooked for opportunities and invitations.

We navigate a world that's not always accessible,
And we're expected to be grateful, not objectionable.
But our struggles are real, and they take a toll,
On our physical and mental health, an endless role.

We fight for inclusion and equality,
And for the recognition of our ability.
For we are not defined by our disabilities,
But rather by our unique personalities and capabilities.

The lack of accessibility in healthcare facilities, which can limit the quality and availability of healthcare services for people with disabilities.

The use of forced labor and institutionalization of people with disabilities during times of war and conflict, such as during the Holocaust.

The use of eugenics and selective breeding to eliminate certain traits and conditions associated with disability, which has been criticized for its ethical implications.

The exclusion of people with disabilities from voting and political participation, which can limit their ability to advocate for their rights and interests.

The lack of access to assistive technologies and devices, which can limit the ability of people with disabilities to live independently and participate fully in society.

The use of forced labor camps for people with disabilities in countries such as China, North Korea, and the Soviet Union.

The lack of accessibility in public spaces such as parks, museums, and cultural institutions, which can limit the ability of people with disabilities to participate in cultural and recreational activities.

The lack of representation and visibility of people with disabilities in media and popular culture, which can perpetuate stereotypes and misconceptions.

The use of sterilization and contraception as a means of population control for people with disabilities, particularly in developing countries.

In The Eyes Of Christ

In the eyes of Christ, all are seen with love,
Disability is not a curse from above.
For every child is cherished in His sight,
And in His mercy, there is no wrong or right.

Jesus saw beyond the body's limitations,
His love for all was without reservations.
He taught that we are more than what we seem,
Our worth is not determined by our physical scheme.

To Christ, disability was just another path,
A way for us to grow and face life's wrath.
For in our struggles, we find strength and grace,
And His love will always fill the empty space.

Jesus would say, "In your weakness, you are strong,
For in your heart, My love will always belong.
You are not defined by your disability,
But by the light and love within your ability."

So let us remember, in our hearts and minds,
That every life is precious and divine.
For in the eyes of Christ, there is no difference,
We are all loved, without any preference.

The lack of access to affordable and accessible housing, which can limit the ability of people with disabilities to live independently and participate fully in society.

The use of forced marriages and sexual sterilization of women with disabilities in some societies, which can violate their human rights and reproductive autonomy.

The lack of accessibility in emergency preparedness and disaster response efforts, which can leave people with disabilities particularly vulnerable in times of crisis.

The use of genetic testing and screening to detect and prevent certain conditions associated with disability, which has been criticized for its potential to perpetuate discrimination and stigma.

The lack of access to mental health services and support, particularly in low- and middle-income countries, which can lead to neglect and mistreatment of people with mental illnesses.

The use of "ableist" language and attitudes in everyday discourse, which can perpetuate harmful stereotypes and contribute to systemic discrimination against people with disabilities.

The use of forced institutionalization and sterilization of Indigenous people with disabilities in countries such as Canada and Australia, as part of a broader history of colonialism and oppression.

The exclusion of people with disabilities from participating in sports and athletics, which can limit their opportunities for physical activity and personal achievement.

The use of conversion therapy to "cure" people of their sexual orientation or gender identity, which can result in significant psychological harm and trauma.

The use of "workhouses" and other forms of forced labor for people with disabilities in the United Kingdom, which contributed to social and economic marginalization.

The use of "medical model" approaches to disability, which focus on fixing or curing disabilities rather than addressing the social and environmental factors that contribute to disability.

The lack of accessibility in information and communication technologies, which can limit the ability of people with disabilities to access information and participate in online communities.

Ramps And Stairs

Ramps and stairs, doors and aisles,
Seemingly simple, but so many trials.
For those with disabilities, they're a wall,
An obstacle that makes their progress crawl.

Lack of accessibility, a painful reality,
A barrier that limits their mobility.
Inaccessible spaces, a constant fight,
A struggle to access, day and night.

From buildings to transport, and every place between,
Lack of accessibility, a constant unseen.
A lack of ramps, lifts or adequate space,
Make it hard for them to join the race.

Their needs are simple, but often ignored,
Their requests unanswered, their voices deplored.
They seek inclusion, they seek respect,
Their struggle for accessibility, they will not neglect.

For every door that's closed, they'll open a new one,
For every step they can't take, they'll rise to the sun.
They'll fight for rights, for dignity and care,
Their spirit and courage, beyond compare.

So let us join them, in the fight for accessibility,
Let us work together, with love and humility.
Let us create a world, where every space is bright,
Where accessibility is a given, a simple right.

The use of physical punishment and abuse as a means of discipline in residential schools and other institutions for children with disabilities.

The lack of accessibility in the criminal justice system, which can lead to wrongful convictions and mistreatment of people with disabilities.

The use of forced institutionalization and electroshock therapy for people with developmental disabilities in countries such as the United States, which led to widespread public outcry and calls for reform.

The lack of representation and leadership of people with disabilities in government, academia, and other sectors, which can perpetuate systemic discrimination and exclusion.

My Wheelchair

My wheelchair, my faithful steed,
Carries me through the world with speed.
With each push of its sturdy wheels,
My heart sings with joy that it feels.

Some see it as a symbol of strife,
A burden, a constant reminder of life.
But to me, it's so much more,
A tool to explore and adore.

My chair, with its comforting embrace,
Allows me to move with ease and grace.
It's not a limitation, but a key,
Unlocking a world that is meant for me.

As I look upon my chair with pride,
I know it is my faithful guide.
Together, we'll face life with a smile,
Overcoming every obstacle, every trial.

So let the world look on with pity,
I'll keep pushing, with fierce tenacity.
For in my chair, I find my wings,
And with them, I soar and sing.

How was disability viewed in prehistoric times?

There is limited evidence on how disability was viewed in prehistoric times, as there are few written records from that era. However, archaeologists and anthropologists have studied prehistoric remains and artifacts to gain some insights into how disabled individuals were treated in these societies.

Some studies suggest that prehistoric societies may have had varying attitudes towards disability, depending on the individual's condition and the society's cultural and social norms. For example, some burials from the Upper Paleolithic period have been found to include individuals with physical impairments, suggesting that they were not abandoned or left to die. In some cases, disabled individuals were buried with valuable artifacts, indicating that they held an important social status in their communities.

On the other hand, other evidence suggests that some prehistoric societies may have practiced infanticide or abandonment of disabled children. For example, skeletal remains of children with congenital disabilities have been found in ancient graves, suggesting that they may have been killed shortly after birth.

Overall, the limited evidence suggests that prehistoric societies had a range of attitudes towards disability, and it likely varied from region to region and depending on the specific disability. It is also important to note that our understanding of prehistoric societies is limited, and much of what we know is based on incomplete evidence and interpretation.

How was disability viewed two thousand years ago?

Two thousand years ago, disability was viewed differently depending on the society and cultural context. In ancient times, people had limited knowledge of the causes and nature of disabilities, and often attributed them to supernatural or divine forces.

In Ancient Greece, disability was often associated with physical imperfections and was considered a sign of weakness and inferiority. Disabled individuals were often excluded from public life and activities, and were not considered suitable for military service or political positions. However, some disabled individuals, such as the philosopher Socrates who was said to have had a physical impairment, were respected for their wisdom and intellect.

In contrast, in Ancient Rome, there were laws protecting the rights of disabled individuals, and some were even employed as performers or in public office. However, this was not a universal practice, and disabled individuals still faced significant challenges in Roman society.

In some ancient cultures, disabled individuals were seen as cursed or possessed by evil spirits. This belief was prevalent in many societies throughout history and often led to the mistreatment and isolation of disabled individuals.

Despite the different attitudes towards disability in ancient times, there were some notable examples of disabled individuals who achieved great accomplishments and recognition. For example, in China, the philosopher Confucius was said to have had a speech impediment, but his teachings and ideas had a profound impact on Chinese culture and society. In India, the emperor Ashoka, who is regarded as one of the greatest rulers in Indian history, was said to have had a physical impairment.

Every Morning

I wake up every morning, with a weight on my chest,
A fear of the world, and what it may do next.
For I know that out there, in the great unknown,
Are people who see me as less than their own.

They see my disability, my differences so clear,
And they judge me without knowing, without a care.
They see me as broken, as someone to be pitied,
As a problem to be solved, rather than a person with dignity.

They whisper behind my back, and stare as I pass,
And I wonder if they see me as something less.
I feel their cold stares, and their unspoken words,
And it hurts more than they'll ever know, or ever could.

But I carry on, with a strength that comes from deep within,
With a resilience that's born from the pain of living.
For I know that I am more than they could ever see,
That my worth and my value, go far beyond my disability.

I am strong, and I am brave,
And I know that I am more than the judgment they gave.
For I am a person, with a heart and a soul,
And I will not let their negativity take control.

So I hold my head high, and I walk with pride,
Knowing that their judgment will never divide.
For I am who I am, solid and to the ground,
And I will never let their negativity bring me down.

What are considered disabilities today?

There are many different types of disabilities that can affect people today. Here are some of the major categories:

Physical disabilities: These are disabilities that affect a person's physical abilities or mobility, such as paralysis, limb amputation, and cerebral palsy.

Sensory disabilities: These are disabilities that affect a person's senses, such as blindness, deafness, and hearing loss.

Intellectual disabilities: These are disabilities that affect a person's cognitive abilities, such as intellectual disability and Down syndrome.

Developmental disabilities: These are disabilities that affect a person's development, such as autism spectrum disorder and attention deficit hyperactivity disorder (ADHD).

Mental health disabilities: These are disabilities that affect a person's mental health and well-being, such as depression, anxiety, and bipolar disorder.

Chronic health conditions: These are conditions that affect a person's health over a long period of time, such as diabetes, asthma, and multiple sclerosis.

Learning disabilities: These are disabilities that affect a person's ability to learn and process information, such as dyslexia and dyscalculia.

Communication disabilities: These are disabilities that affect a person's ability to communicate effectively, such as stuttering and aphasia.

It is important to note that many people may experience multiple disabilities, and that the impact of disabilities can vary widely depending on a range of individual and environmental factors. Furthermore, disability is a complex and diverse phenomenon that requires a holistic and inclusive approach to understanding and addressing the needs and experiences of individuals with disabilities.

Test yourself with these true or false questions:
Answers appear on the next page.

1. The only way to help people with disabilities is through medical interventions or cures.
2. People with disabilities cannot have successful careers or businesses.
3. Disability is always permanent and cannot be improved.
4. People with disabilities are always a burden on their families and caregivers.
5. Disability is only relevant to the health and medical fields.
6. People with disabilities are less valuable or less important than non-disabled people.
7. Disability is always associated with weakness or vulnerability.
8. People with disabilities cannot travel or explore the world.
9. Disability is always a barrier to education and learning.
10. People with disabilities are always dependent on government assistance.
11. Disability is always visible from birth or childhood.
12. People with disabilities are more likely to experience social isolation and loneliness.
13. Disability is always a personal tragedy that cannot be overcome.
14. People with disabilities are more likely to experience poverty and financial hardship.
15. Disability is always a negative and unwanted aspect of life.

Answers:

1. F
2. F
3. F
4. F
5. F
6. F
7. F
8. F
9. F
10. F
11. F
12. T
13. F
14. T
15. F

Disability Culture Is A Tapestry

Disability culture is a tapestry woven strong,
A celebration of difference, a triumph over wrong.
For in this culture, we find beauty in every form,
And honor the strength that each unique identity is born.

It is a culture that embraces all abilities,
And finds power in our shared vulnerabilities.
For we all face challenges, obstacles to overcome,
And it is through our struggles that our community is won.

Disability culture is a rich and vibrant song,
A melody that sings of the places we belong.
For in this culture, we find acceptance and love,
And a recognition of the power in being enough.

It is a culture that teaches us empathy and care,
And encourages us to reach out and share.
For we are all part of a greater whole,
And it is through our differences that we find our soul.

Disability culture is a dance that we all can learn,
A celebration of every step and every turn.
For in this culture, we find hope and inspiration,
And a recognition of the beauty in our shared creation.

So let us embrace disability culture, one and all,
And celebrate the strength in every rise and fall.
For in our differences, we find our greatest wealth,
And in our diversity, we find our shared health.

What is disability culture?

Disability culture refers to the unique and shared experiences, traditions, values, and perspectives of people with disabilities. It is a community that has its own history, art, language, and social norms. Disability culture is shaped by the experiences of living with a disability and the ways in which people with disabilities interact with each other and the world around them.

Disability culture is an important part of the larger disability rights movement. It celebrates the diversity and strengths of people with disabilities and challenges the ableist assumptions and stereotypes that are often associated with disability. Disability culture values accessibility, inclusion, and the unique contributions that people with disabilities bring to society.

Some examples of disability culture include:

Disability pride: The idea that having a disability is something to be celebrated, rather than something to be ashamed of.

Disability arts: Artistic expressions by people with disabilities, including visual art, literature, theater, and music.

Disability language: Language used by people with disabilities to describe themselves and their experiences.

This can include terms such as "ableism," "accessibility," and "invisible disability."

Disability history: The history of disability rights and advocacy, including the fight for accessibility, inclusion, and equal rights.

Disability community: The social connections and networks of people with disabilities, including support groups, online communities, and disability-led organizations.

Overall, disability culture is a way for people with disabilities to celebrate their unique experiences, connect with others who share those experiences, and challenge the ableist attitudes and systems that can make life more difficult for people with disabilities.

What is the history of disability culture?

The history of disability culture is complex and multifaceted, encompassing a range of different experiences and perspectives. Disability culture refers to the unique social, artistic, and political movements that have emerged from the experiences of people with disabilities throughout history. These movements have sought to challenge ableist attitudes and structures in society, promote greater accessibility and inclusion, and celebrate the diversity and richness of disabled experiences.

One of the earliest examples of disability culture can be traced back to ancient civilizations such as Greece and Rome, where disabled people were often viewed as objects of pity or scorn. However, there were also instances of disabled individuals being celebrated for their unique talents and abilities, such as the blind poet Homer.

In the medieval period, disabled people were often excluded from society and treated as outcasts. However, there were also instances of disabled individuals being valued for their religious or spiritual insights, such as the medieval mystic Julian of Norwich.

During the Enlightenment, disabled people were often seen as inferior or defective, and were subjected to medicalization and institutionalization. However, there were also instances of disabled people advocating for their rights and dignity, such as the 18th century philosopher and writer Diderot.

In the 20th century, disability culture began to emerge as a distinct movement, with disabled people coming together to challenge stereotypes and advocate for greater inclusion and accessibility. The disability rights movement of the 1960s and 1970s played a particularly significant role in promoting disability culture, with activists working to change laws and attitudes that perpetuated discrimination and exclusion.

Today, disability culture continues to evolve and grow, with disabled artists, writers, and activists creating and sharing their work through various mediums such as social media and digital platforms. The disability pride movement, which celebrates the unique identities and experiences of disabled people, has also gained momentum in recent years.

We Are A Community

We are a community, diverse and strong,
Our lives shaped by disability all along.
We celebrate the things that make us unique,
Our differences are not something to critique.

We have a culture, born from shared experience,
A history of advocacy, of rights and persistence.
Our language, our art, our stories to be told,
All reflecting the beauty that we hold.

We have our heroes, our leaders and guides,
Who fought for our rights, and pushed aside,
The ableist views that tried to control,
And tried to keep us from reaching our goals.

We have our language, a vocabulary all our own,
Words like "accessibility" and "ableism" we've grown.
We use them to describe the world around us,
And the challenges we face that can frustrate and fuss.

We have our arts, our music and dance,
A way to express ourselves, to take a chance.
We create beauty out of our struggles and pain,
And find joy and connection is what we gain.

We have our community, our support and care,
A place where we can be ourselves, and share,
Our experiences and our hopes and fears,
And find comfort and strength through our peers.

We are a culture, with stories to tell,
Of a life that is different, but still just as swell.
We are a community, full of resilience and grace,
And we celebrate our differences, in every single place.

Homer

Homer was an ancient Greek poet who is believed to have lived in the 8th century BCE, although little is known for certain about his life. He is famous for his epic poems, the Iliad and the Odyssey, which are among the most important works of literature in Western civilization.

According to legend, Homer was blind, although this has been debated by scholars. He is thought to have been born in either Chios or Smyrna, both of which were important centers of Greek culture at the time.

The Iliad and the Odyssey are both epic poems that tell the stories of heroes and gods in ancient Greece. The Iliad focuses on the Trojan War, in which the Greeks fought against the Trojans for 10 years, while the Odyssey tells the story of the Greek hero Odysseus as he journeys home after the war.

Homer's works were hugely influential in ancient Greece and were performed in public by actors and musicians. They were also widely read and studied, and have been translated into many different languages over the centuries.

Although the exact details of Homer's life are unclear, his legacy as a poet and storyteller has endured through the ages. He is considered one of the greatest poets in Western literature, and his works continue to be read and studied by scholars and enthusiasts alike.

Julian of Norwich

Julian of Norwich (1342-1416) was a medieval English mystic and writer known for her spiritual insights and teachings on the nature of God's love and compassion. She is one of the earliest known female authors in the English language and is revered as a saint by many Christian denominations.

Little is known about Julian's early life, including her birthplace and family background. She lived during a time of great social and political upheaval in England, including the Black Death and the Hundred Years' War.

At the age of 30, Julian became gravely ill and received a series of 16 visions or "showings" of Jesus Christ that she believed came directly from God. These visions, which she recorded in her book "Revelations of Divine Love," formed the basis of her spiritual teachings and writings.

In her book, Julian emphasized the boundless love and compassion of God, whom she referred to as a mother figure. She wrote that God's love is always present and available to all people, regardless of their sins or shortcomings, and that all human beings have the potential to experience this love and achieve spiritual union with God.

Julian's teachings were considered radical for her time, as they challenged traditional Christian doctrines and emphasized the importance of personal experience and individual revelation. She also advocated for the role of women in the church, and her writings have been seen as an early feminist critique of patriarchal religious structures.

Despite facing opposition from some religious authorities, Julian's teachings gained a following among both laypeople and clergy. She continued to live a life of contemplation and prayer, eventually becoming an anchoress (a type of religious hermit) and residing in a small cell attached to a church in Norwich, England.

Julian's legacy as a spiritual leader and writer has endured through the centuries, with her writings continuing to inspire and influence people of all faiths today.

Denis Diderot

Denis Diderot (1713-1784) was a French philosopher, writer, and encyclopedist who was a leading figure of the Enlightenment. While Diderot did not focus specifically on disability issues, he was a strong advocate for the rights and dignity of all human beings, regardless of their social status or physical abilities.

Diderot's most famous work, the Encyclopédie, was a monumental project aimed at compiling and disseminating knowledge in a wide range of fields, from science and philosophy to art and politics. The Encyclopédie included articles on disability and related topics, such as medicine, anatomy, and psychology.

Diderot also wrote extensively about the importance of education and access to knowledge for all individuals, regardless of their background or abilities. He believed that education was the key to social and political progress, and he advocated for the establishment of schools and universities that were open to everyone, including disabled people.

In addition, Diderot was a vocal critic of the oppressive social structures that kept people marginalized and excluded from society. He believed that all individuals had the right to autonomy and self-determination, and he called for the abolition of slavery, serfdom, and other forms of exploitation and oppression.

Although Diderot did not focus specifically on disability issues, his broader advocacy for human rights and dignity laid the groundwork for later disability rights movements. Today, his writings continue to inspire people around the world who are working to create a more just and equitable society for all individuals, including those with disabilities.

What do disabled people value?

Disabled people, like any other group of people, have a wide range of values and beliefs that are unique to their individual experiences and identities. However, there are some common values that many disabled people share. Here are a few examples:

Accessibility and inclusion: Disabled people often value the ability to participate fully in all aspects of society, including work, education, social activities, and public spaces. They value accommodations and accessibility measures that help them do so.

Autonomy and independence: Many disabled people value the ability to make their own choices and decisions, and to live as independently as possible. They may value supports and accommodations that help them achieve this. Diversity and representation: Disabled people value diversity and the recognition that disability is not a one-size-fits-all experience. They value representation in media and other areas of society, and the ability to see themselves reflected positively in the world around them.

Community and connection: Many disabled people value the connections they have with other disabled people and the sense of community that comes with shared experiences. They may also value the support of family and friends.

Empowerment and advocacy: Disabled people often value the ability to advocate for themselves and others, and to work towards greater inclusion and accessibility in society. They may also value the empowerment that comes with speaking out about their experiences and challenging ableist attitudes and stereotypes

Overall, disabled people value the same things as anyone else - love, respect, dignity, and the ability to live a fulfilling life. However, the experience of disability can shape and influence these values in unique and important ways.

Stereotypes Of Disabled People

Unfortunately, disabled people are often subjected to various stereotypes and misconceptions, including:

Helpless and dependent: The stereotype that all disabled people are helpless and dependent on others for basic tasks or activities.

Inspirational and brave: The stereotype that disabled people are always brave and inspiring simply because of their disability, rather than for their actual accomplishments or character.

Pitiable and tragic: The stereotype that disabled people are to be pitied and seen as tragic figures, rather than as full and complex human beings.

Burden on society: The stereotype that disabled people are a burden on society, requiring extra resources and accommodations that others must pay for.

Asexual or hypersexual: The stereotype that disabled people are either asexual or overly sexual, and that their sexuality is somehow abnormal or deviant.

Abnormal or broken: The stereotype that disabled people are abnormal or broken in some way, and that their disability is a flaw or defect that needs to be fixed.

Unintelligent or incompetent: The stereotype that disabled people are unintelligent or incompetent, and unable to contribute meaningfully to society.

It's important to recognize that these stereotypes are harmful and often inaccurate, and to work towards challenging and dismantling them in our attitudes and behaviors towards disabled people.

False Assumptions About Disabled People

It's important to recognize that disabled people are often subjected to untrue or harmful assumptions, misconceptions, or stereotypes. Here are a few examples:

All disabled people are the same: This is simply not true. Disability is a diverse and complex experience that can manifest in a wide variety of ways, and each disabled person has their own unique experiences and identities.

Disabled people are always in pain: While chronic pain can be a part of some disabilities, it is not a universal experience. Many disabled people do not experience chronic pain, and assuming that they do can be harmful and dismissive.

Disabled people are asexual: Disabled people have the same range of sexual orientations and desires as non-disabled people, and assuming otherwise is not only untrue but also reinforces harmful stereotypes.

Disabled people cannot have fulfilling lives: This is a harmful and untrue assumption. Disabled people can and do lead fulfilling and meaningful lives, with rich relationships, hobbies, careers, and experiences.

Disabled people are a burden on society: This is a harmful and untrue stereotype that devalues the contributions and humanity of disabled people. Disabled people can and do contribute meaningfully to society in a variety of ways, and deserve to be recognized and valued for their contributions.

Disabled people are not as smart or competent as non-disabled people: This is simply not true. Disabled people have a wide range of abilities, and many excel in areas such as science, technology, arts, and sports.

It's important to challenge these and other untrue assumptions about disabled people, and to recognize that disability is a diverse and complex experience that deserves to be valued and respected.

What are the pros and cons of keeping severely disabled people alive?

The decision to keep severely disabled people alive is a complex and often difficult one. There are pros and cons to consider, which may vary depending on the individual circumstances. Here are some potential pros and cons to consider.

Pros:

Compassion: Many people believe that it is important to provide care and support to individuals with severe disabilities out of compassion and a desire to ensure their well-being.

Quality of life: Some people with severe disabilities are still able to experience joy and meaningful interactions with others, and they may value the opportunity to continue living despite their challenges.

Medical advances: With advances in medical technology and treatments, some conditions that were once considered fatal may now be treated or managed, giving severely disabled people a chance at a longer life.

Diversity: Including and valuing people with disabilities promotes diversity and inclusion, which can benefit society as a whole.

Cons:

Suffering: Severely disabled individuals may experience significant physical and emotional suffering, which may be difficult to manage and alleviate.

Financial burden: Providing care for severely disabled individuals can be expensive, and the cost may fall on the family or society as a whole.

Quality of life: While some people with severe disabilities may value life, others may feel that their quality of life is poor and that they would prefer not to continue living.

Ethical concerns: Some people may believe that it is not ethical to prolong the life of severely disabled individuals who may not be able to experience the fullness of life.

In conclusion, the decision to keep severely disabled people alive is a complex one that requires careful consideration of the pros and cons. It is important to consider the individual circumstances and to involve the person, their family, and medical professionals in the decision-making process.

We Exist

We want you to know that we exist,
Though sometimes you might forget or dismiss.
We want you to see us as people, whole and complete,
Not defined by our disabilities, or what we cannot do or compete.

We want you to know that we have dreams and goals,
And despite the challenges, we have the strength to unfold.
We want you to believe in our capabilities,
And support us in our quest for true accessibility.

We want you to know that we are a diverse community,
And disability is just one aspect of our identity.
We want you to see the beauty in our differences,
And celebrate the unique perspectives and experiences we bring.

We want you to know that we are not to be pitied,
Or seen as a burden, a problem, or a liability.
We want you to respect our autonomy and choices,
Our lives are just as valuable as anybody's.

We want you to know that our existence matters,
And our voices should be heard and amplified louder.
We want you to join us in the fight for equity and inclusion,
And create a world where disability is not a source of exclusion.

So listen to us, see us, and believe in us,
And together we can create a world that is just.
A world where we can all thrive and succeed,
And a world where our differences are celebrated indeed.

What can disabled people offer us?

People with disabilities can offer a wealth of skills, knowledge, and perspectives to individuals, organizations, and society as a whole. Here are some examples:

Unique perspectives: People with disabilities often have unique perspectives and experiences that can enrich our understanding of the world and challenge our assumptions.

Resilience and creativity: Many people with disabilities have developed resilience and creativity in the face of the challenges they have experienced, and can offer valuable insights and solutions in a variety of contexts.

Skills and expertise: People with disabilities have a wide range of skills and expertise, from specialized technical skills to interpersonal and communication skills.

Innovation: Some of the most innovative technologies and products have been developed by people with disabilities to address their own needs, such as text-to-speech software and hearing aids.

Diversity and inclusion: Embracing diversity and inclusion is important for any organization or community, and including people with disabilities can help foster a more inclusive and welcoming environment for everyone.

It's important to recognize that people with disabilities should not be seen solely as a source of inspiration or as objects of charity, but rather as valued members of society who have a lot to offer. Providing opportunities and accommodations for people with disabilities to fully participate in all aspects of life can benefit everyone.

A Gift

In every way, in every form,
Disabled people offer us a gift.
Their strength, their spirit, their love so warm,
Their resilience is what gives us lift.

They teach us patience, they teach us grace,
They show us how to persevere.
Their struggles make us look at life's face,
In a different way, with a new clear.

They offer us a perspective unique,
Their lived experiences, their perspective true.
Their stories enlighten, our hearts they pique,
Their presence enriches all we do.

They offer us creativity, they offer us art,
Their minds are sharp, their souls are pure.
They remind us that life is a work of art,
And we must embrace every color and hue.

They teach us kindness, they teach us care,
Their hearts are open, their souls are pure.
They remind us that love is always there,
And it's the one thing that will always endure.

So let us honor them, let us give thanks,
For all the gifts that they impart.
For their lives enrich ours in every way,
And they inspire us with their brave hearts.

What are the issues affecting disabled people today?

There are many issues that affect disabled people today, both at the individual and societal levels. Here are some of the major issues:

Accessibility: Many disabled people face barriers to accessing physical environments, transportation, information, and communication. This can limit their participation in society and make it difficult for them to live independently.

Discrimination: Disabled people may face discrimination and prejudice in many areas of life, including employment, education, and healthcare. This can limit their opportunities and contribute to social exclusion.

Poverty: Disabled people are more likely to live in poverty than non-disabled people, due to factors such as discrimination, barriers to education and employment, and limited access to social services.

Healthcare: Disabled people may face challenges in accessing healthcare services that meet their specific needs, including access to assistive technology, rehabilitation services, and mental healthcare.

Employment: Disabled people may face barriers to employment, including discrimination, lack of accommodations, and limited access to education and training.

Education: Disabled people may face barriers to accessing education that meets their specific needs, including access to assistive technology, accommodations, and specialized teachers.

Social isolation: Disabled people may experience social isolation and loneliness, due to barriers to participation in social activities and limited access to transportation

Violence and abuse: Disabled people are at higher risk of experiencing violence and abuse, including physical, sexual, and emotional abuse, as well as neglect.

It is important to recognize that these issues are complex and interrelated, and that addressing them requires a comprehensive and holistic approach that takes into account the diversity and complexity of disability experiences.

What barriers do disabled people face today?

Despite the progress made in recognizing the rights of people with disabilities, there are still many barriers that they face today. These barriers can be physical, social, economic, or cultural in nature. Here are some examples:

Physical Barriers: Physical barriers can include inaccessible buildings, transportation, and public spaces. People with mobility impairments may find it difficult or impossible to access these places, limiting their ability to participate fully in society.

Attitudinal Barriers: Attitudinal barriers refer to the negative attitudes and stereotypes that people with disabilities face. These can lead to discrimination and exclusion, making it harder for people with disabilities to find employment, housing, and healthcare.

Economic Barriers: People with disabilities are more likely to experience poverty and unemployment than the general population. This can be due to a lack of access to education and training, as well as discrimination in the workplace.

Social and Cultural Barriers: Social and cultural barriers can include the lack of representation of people with disabilities in the media and popular culture, as well as the stigma and discrimination they may face in their personal relationships.

Communication Barriers: People with hearing, speech, or visual impairments may face communication barriers that limit their ability to interact with others, access information, or participate in activities.

Legal and Policy Barriers: Despite laws and policies designed to protect the rights of people with disabilities, there are still gaps in enforcement and accessibility. This can lead to further exclusion and discrimination.

It is important to recognize these barriers and work to remove them to ensure that people with disabilities have the same opportunities and rights as everyone else.

They Will Not Rest

They march with pride, they stand so tall,
Their voices raised, their message clear.
They fight for rights, for one and all,
For those with disabilities, far and near.

They will not rest, they will not yield,
Their cause is just, their hearts are pure.
They'll break down barriers, they'll never shield,
Their determination will forever endure.

They face discrimination every day,
They struggle to be seen and heard.
But they will not let society sway,
Their voices will be their sword.

They seek accessibility, they seek respect,
They seek inclusion in every way.
Their battle will not end until they collect,
Their rights, their dignity, every day.

So let us join them, let us stand as one,
With those who are disabled, let us fight.
Let's work together until it's done,
Until every barrier is out of sight.

For they are the heroes, the champions of the hour,
Who fight for what is right, for justice and power.
So let us lift them up, let us raise their voice,
For they deserve equality, it's their right and choice.

Which countries promote disability rights?

Many countries around the world have made significant efforts to promote disability rights and improve the lives of people with disabilities. Here are a few examples:

United States: The Americans with Disabilities Act (ADA) is a federal law that prohibits discrimination against people with disabilities in all areas of public life, including employment, education, transportation, and public accommodations. The ADA has been a model for disability rights legislation around the world.

United Kingdom: The UK has a strong legal framework for disability rights, including the Equality Act 2010, which protects people with disabilities from discrimination in employment, education, and other areas. The government also provides financial support and services to help people with disabilities live independently.

Canada: Canada has a national strategy for disability inclusion, which aims to remove barriers and increase accessibility for people with disabilities. The country also has strong anti-discrimination laws, including the Canadian Human Rights Act.

Sweden: Sweden has a comprehensive social welfare system that provides support and services for people with disabilities, including healthcare, education, and employment services. The country has also made significant efforts to promote accessibility in public spaces and transportation.

Australia: Australia has a Disability Discrimination Act that prohibits discrimination against people with disabilities in all areas of public life. The government provides financial support and services to help people with disabilities live independently, and has also made efforts to promote accessibility and inclusion in public spaces.

Norway: Norway has a comprehensive social welfare system that provides support and services for people with disabilities, including healthcare, education, and employment services.

Germany: Germany has strong anti-discrimination laws, including the General Equal Treatment Act, which prohibits discrimination based on disability in all areas of public life.

Japan: Japan has made significant efforts to promote accessibility and inclusion for people with disabilities, including improving public transportation and providing financial support for accessibility upgrades.

New Zealand: New Zealand has a Disability Strategy that aims to remove barriers and increase accessibility for people with disabilities. The country also has strong anti-discrimination laws, including the Human Rights Act.

Brazil: Brazil has a national policy for the inclusion of people with disabilities that aims to improve accessibility, provide education and employment opportunities, and increase social inclusion.

South Korea: South Korea has made efforts to promote accessibility and inclusion for people with disabilities, including providing financial support for accessibility upgrades and improving public transportation.

Spain: Spain has a strong legal framework for disability rights, including the Law on Social Integration of People with Disabilities and the Equal Opportunities, Non-Discrimination and Universal Accessibility Law.

Thank You, Dear Countries

Thank you, dear countries, for your human rights,
For upholding justice and treating all with might,
For recognizing the value of every life,
And striving to end all forms of strife.

Thank you for supporting the disabled,
For recognizing their needs, and being able,
To provide them with access to education,
Healthcare, and employment without hesitation.

Thank you for creating a world that's inclusive,
Where people of all abilities can be productive,
Where everyone has a chance to succeed,
And their contributions are valued indeed.

Thank you for showing that disability is not a weakness,
But a unique strength that adds to life's richness,
For breaking down barriers and removing the stigma,
And creating a world that's more loving and bigger.

So let us continue to work together,
To ensure that everyone has equal access to the treasure,
Of human rights and opportunities,
And make this world a better place for all communities.

Finland: Finland has a comprehensive social welfare system that provides support and services for people with disabilities, including healthcare, education, and employment services.

Ireland: Ireland has a National Disability Inclusion Strategy that aims to improve accessibility, increase employment opportunities, and promote social inclusion for people with disabilities.

Mexico: Mexico has a national disability law that aims to improve accessibility, provide education and employment opportunities, and increase social inclusion for people with disabilities.

Denmark: Denmark has a strong legal framework for disability rights, including the Act on Prohibition of Discrimination Based on Disability and the Act on Social Services.

France: France has a national plan for the inclusion of people with disabilities that aims to improve accessibility, provide education and employment opportunities, and increase social inclusion.

Italy: Italy has a national strategy for the inclusion of people with disabilities that aims to improve accessibility, provide education and employment opportunities, and increase social inclusion.

Israel: Israel has made efforts to promote accessibility and inclusion for people with disabilities, including providing financial support for accessibility upgrades and improving public transportation.

Argentina: Argentina has a national disability law that aims to improve accessibility, provide education and employment opportunities, and increase social inclusion for people with disabilities.

Portugal: Portugal has a strong legal framework for disability rights, including the Law on the Rights of People with Disabilities and the National Plan for the Promotion of the Rights of People with Disabilities.

Switzerland: Switzerland has a comprehensive social welfare system that provides support and services for people with disabilities, including healthcare, education, and employment services.

South Africa: South Africa has a White Paper on the Rights of Persons with Disabilities that aims to improve accessibility, provide education and employment opportunities, and increase social inclusion.

Netherlands: The Netherlands has a strong legal framework for disability rights, including the Equal Treatment Act and the Social Support Act.

Austria: Austria has a comprehensive social welfare system that provides support and services for people with disabilities, including healthcare, education, and employment services. The country also has strong anti-discrimination laws.

Which countries treat disabled people badly?

It's important to note that the treatment of disabled people can vary widely within any country, and it is not appropriate to generalize the treatment of disabled people in any given country. However, there are some countries where disabled people face significant challenges and barriers to their inclusion and well-being. Some of these countries include:

Afghanistan: In Afghanistan, disabled people face discrimination, social stigma, and limited access to healthcare, education, and employment.

North Korea: Disabled people in North Korea face discrimination and social stigma, and are often excluded from mainstream society. The government does not provide adequate support or services for people with disabilities.

Saudi Arabia, Somalia, Zimbabwe, Myanmar, Iran, Egypt, Nigeria, Pakistan, Russia, Yemen, Cambodia, Haiti: Disabled people in Saudi Arabia face significant challenges in accessing education, employment, and healthcare. They also face discrimination and social stigma.

Syria: Disabled people in Syria have been disproportionately affected by the ongoing conflict, with many lacking access to basic services and support.

Venezuela: Disabled people in Venezuela face significant challenges in accessing healthcare and basic services, as well as discrimination and social stigma.

Iraq: Disabled people in Iraq have been disproportionately affected by the ongoing conflict, with many lacking access to basic services and support.

It's important to note that this is not an exhaustive list, and there are likely many other countries where disabled people face significant challenges and barriers. It is important for governments, organizations, and individuals to work together to promote disability rights and inclusion worldwide.

In The Eyes Of A Mother
Part 2

She sees the world in a different light,
Through her child's eyes and heart,
And knows that life is so more than what we see,
It's about living every moment with purpose and art.

So, she holds her child close,
And whispers words of love and inspiration,
For she knows that in this child's heart,
Lies a true gift to the entire nation.

A child with a heart so pure,
A spirit that knows no bounds,
A spirit that shines like a star,
And a love that forever astounds.

In the eyes of a mother,
A disabled child is not a flaw,
But a true gift from above,
A miracle to love and adore.

Test yourself with these true or false questions:

Answers appear on the next page.

1. People with disabilities cannot have active and fulfilling social lives.
2. Disability is always a burden on society and the economy.
3. People with disabilities cannot have fulfilling and satisfying sex lives.
4. Disability is always a result of individual failings or shortcomings.
5. People with disabilities cannot have successful and happy marriages.
6. Disability is always associated with shame and embarrassment.
7. People with disabilities cannot participate in cultural or artistic activities.
8. Disability is always a result of accidents or injuries.
9. People with disabilities cannot be independent and self-sufficient.
10. Disability is always a barrier to social and economic success.
11. People with disabilities cannot have children or be good parents.
12. People with disabilities always need help or assistance.
13. Disabled people have made significant contributions to society.
14. Anyone can become disabled at any time.
15. Some disabilities can be overcome or prevented.

Answers:

1. F
2. F
3. F
4. F
5. F
6. F
7. F
8. F
9. F
10. F
11. F
12. F
13. T
14. T
15. T

In A World Full Of Stars

In a world full of stars and endless skies,
Stephen Hawking soared, defying all the lies.
For though his body was wracked with disability,
His mind soared beyond what most could see.

In a wheelchair, he traversed the world,
A mind full of brilliance, his flag unfurled.
For though his body may have been weak,
His mind was strong, full of knowledge to seek.

He taught us all to reach for the stars,
To push beyond our limitations and scars.
For though our bodies may falter and fail,
Our minds can soar beyond any veil.

He changed the world with his brilliant mind,
Pushing the limits of what we thought we could find.
For he showed us that disability is no bar,
To reaching for the heavens, near or far.

In his legacy, we find hope and inspiration,
And a call to embrace our own determination.
For in our differences, we find our strength,
And in our diversity, we find our depth.

So let us remember Stephen Hawking's name,
And honor the legacy of his brilliant brain.
For in his disability, he showed us all,
The power of the human spirit, standing tall.

Disability Champions

There are many famous disabled people who have made significant contributions to promoting disability rights and raising awareness about disability issues. Here are some examples:

Stephen Hawking: Hawking was a renowned physicist and author who had ALS, a progressive neurodegenerative disease. He used his platform to raise awareness about the challenges faced by people with disabilities and was an advocate for accessible education and healthcare.

Marlee Matlin: Matlin is an Academy Award-winning actress who is deaf. She has used her platform to advocate for deaf rights and promote accessibility in the entertainment industry.

Frida Kahlo: Kahlo was a Mexican artist who had polio as a child and later suffered a debilitating injury in a bus accident. She used her art to express her experiences as a disabled person and challenge societal norms around disability.

Temple Grandin: Grandin is a renowned animal behaviorist who has autism. She has used her platform to raise awareness about the strengths and talents of people with autism and promote understanding and acceptance.

Helen Keller: Keller was a renowned author and activist who was deaf and blind. She used her platform to advocate for the rights of people with disabilities and promote accessible education and employment.

John Hockenberry: Hockenberry is a journalist and author who uses a wheelchair due to a spinal cord injury.

He has used his platform to raise awareness about disability issues and advocate for accessibility and inclusion.

Michael J. Fox: Fox is an actor and advocate who has Parkinson's disease. He has used his platform to raise awareness about the challenges faced by people with Parkinson's and promote research and advocacy.

Tammy Duckworth: Duckworth is a United States Senator and veteran who lost both her legs in combat. She has used her platform to advocate for veterans' rights and promote accessibility and inclusion for people with disabilities

Ed Roberts: Roberts was a disability rights activist who had polio and used a wheelchair. He founded the Center for Independent Living and was a pioneer in the disability rights movement.

Let Us Celebrate

Let us celebrate the beauty of disability,
For it is a part of our human diversity.
Let us embrace the differences that we see,
And cherish every unique identity.

For disability is not a flaw or mistake,
But a part of what makes us truly great.
It teaches us empathy, love, and grace,
And reveals the strength in every face.

Let us celebrate the beauty of every ability,
And honor the unique stories that we bring.
For disability is not a sign of frailty,
But a testament to the power of being.

Let us dance to the beat of a different drum,
And find joy in the things that make us one.
For in our differences, we find unity,
And in our humanity, we find community.

So let us celebrate the beauty of disability,
And honor the strength in every identity.
For in our uniqueness, we find beauty,
And in our diversity, we find our unity.

Haben Girma: Girma is a disability rights advocate and attorney who is deaf/blind. She has used her platform to advocate for accessible education and employment, and was the first deaf/blind person to graduate from Harvard Law School.

Neil Marcus: Marcus is a writer and performance artist who has cerebral palsy. He has used his art to challenge societal norms around disability and promote accessibility and inclusion.

Andrea Bocelli: Bocelli is an Italian singer who is blind. He has used his platform to raise awareness about blindness and promote accessible music education and performance.

Stella Young: Young was an Australian comedian and disability rights activist who had osteogenesis imperfecta, a genetic disorder that results in brittle bones. She used her platform to challenge ableism and promote accessibility and inclusion.

Christy Brown: Brown was an Irish writer and artist who had cerebral palsy. He used his art to express his experiences as a disabled person and challenge societal norms around disability.

Judy Heumann: Heumann is a disability rights advocate who has spinal cord injury. She has used her platform to advocate for accessible education and employment, and was instrumental in the development of the Americans with Disabilities Act.

Warwick Davis: Davis is an actor and advocate who has dwarfism. He has used his platform to raise awareness about the challenges faced by people with dwarfism and promote accessible entertainment.

Maysoon Zayid: Zayid is a comedian and disability rights advocate who has cerebral palsy. She has used her platform to challenge ableism and promote accessibility and inclusion.

Tanni Grey-Thompson: Grey-Thompson is a retired Paralympic athlete and advocate who has spina bifida. She has used her platform to advocate for accessible sports and promote understanding and acceptance of disability.

These are just a few examples of the many famous disabled people who have made significant contributions to promoting disability rights and awareness.

Famous people who we did not know have disabilities.

There are many famous people who have disabilities that may not be widely known. Here are some examples:

Selena Gomez: Gomez is a singer and actress who has lupus, an autoimmune disease.

Gal Gadot: Gadot is an actress who played Wonder Woman in the DC Extended Universe films. She has partial paralysis on the left side of her face due to a nerve injury.

Tommy Hilfiger: Hilfiger is a fashion designer who has dyslexia.

Lady Gaga: Gaga is a singer and actress who has fibromyalgia, a chronic pain condition.

Whoopi Goldberg: Goldberg is an actress and talk show host who has dyslexia.

Tommy Edison: Edison is a YouTube personality who has been blind since birth. He has a popular YouTube channel where he talks about his experiences as a blind person.

Anderson Cooper: Cooper is a journalist and television personality who has dyslexia.

Adam Levine: Levine is a singer and songwriter who has attention deficit hyperactivity disorder (ADHD).

Daniel Radcliffe: Radcliffe is an actor who played Harry Potter in the film series. He has dyspraxia, a developmental coordination disorder.

Christopher Reeve: Reeve was an actor who played Superman in the 1970s and 80s. He became quadriplegic after a horse riding accident in 1995 and became an advocate for spinal cord injury research.

John Nash: Nash was a mathematician who had schizophrenia. He won the Nobel Prize in Economics in 1994 and his life was the subject of the movie "A Beautiful Mind."

Halle Berry: Berry is an actress who has diabetes.

Elton John: John is a singer-songwriter who has had a lifelong battle with addiction and bulimia.

Richard Branson: Branson is a British entrepreneur who has dyslexia. He has used his experiences to promote dyslexia awareness and to encourage alternative approaches to education.

These are just a few examples of the many famous people who have disabilities that may not be widely known. It's important to remember that disability is a natural part of the human experience and can affect anyone, regardless of their background or profession.

What is the economic circumstances of a disabled person versus an able-bodied person?

The economic circumstances of a disabled person are often different from those of an able-bodied person. Disability can significantly impact a person's ability to earn income and maintain financial stability. Here are some ways in which the economic circumstances of a disabled person may differ from an able-bodied person:

Employment: People with disabilities are more likely to be unemployed or underemployed compared to able-bodied individuals. They may face barriers in finding and keeping a job, such as discrimination, inaccessible workplaces, and lack of accommodations.

Income: Disabled people may earn less than able-bodied people, even when they are employed. This wage gap can be due to factors such as discrimination, lower levels of education and training, and the types of jobs that are available to them.

Healthcare Costs: Disabled individuals often require ongoing medical care, which can be expensive. They may have higher out-of-pocket costs for healthcare and may not have access to affordable health insurance.

Social Security Benefits: Many disabled individuals rely on Social Security Disability Insurance (SSDI) or Supplemental Security Income (SSI) for income support. These programs provide financial assistance to those who are unable to work due to a disability, but the benefits are often not enough to cover all expenses.

Overall, disabled individuals are more likely to experience poverty and financial hardship than able-bodied individuals. This can have a significant impact on their quality of life, access to healthcare, and ability to participate fully in society. It is important to recognize and address the economic challenges faced by disabled people in order to promote equity and inclusion.

Tarek the hunter

In a prehistoric tribe, there was a young hunter named Tarek. Tarek had always dreamed of being a great hunter like his father and grandfather before him. However, Tarek was born with a physical disability that prevented him from being able to run or hunt like the other members of his tribe. Tarek felt sad and left out, especially when he saw the other hunters return from their successful hunts with large animals in tow.

Tarek's family noticed how down he was feeling and decided to do something about it. They started to include him in their meals by sharing the meat they had hunted with him. Tarek felt grateful for their kindness but still felt like he was missing out on something.

One day, while the hunters were out on a hunt, Tarek decided to venture out on his own to find some food. He slowly made his way through the forest, using a stick to help him walk. After a while, Tarek stumbled upon a small stream. As he was looking for fish, he noticed a group of birds perched on a nearby tree. Tarek realized that he could use his throwing skills to catch the birds.

He picked up a few stones and started throwing them at the birds. After a few tries, he finally hit one of them. He was ecstatic and quickly picked up the bird. Tarek returned to his tribe, proudly holding up the bird he had caught. His family and the rest of the tribe were amazed at what he had done.

From that day on, Tarek became known as the tribe's bird hunter. He would often venture out on his own to catch birds, which became a valuable addition to the tribe's diet. His family was proud of him and grateful for the new source of food that he had brought to the tribe.

Despite his physical disability, Tarek had found a way to contribute to the tribe and had earned the respect of his fellow hunters. He learned that being different did not mean that he couldn't contribute to his community. He was happy and content knowing that he had found his own way of being a successful hunter, and that his family would always be there to support him.

Disability Rights

There are numerous initiatives, policies, and movements taking place around the world to promote disability rights. Here are a few specific examples:

The United Nations Convention on the Rights of Persons with Disabilities (CRPD): The CRPD is an international treaty that sets out the rights of people with disabilities and promotes their full inclusion in all aspects of society. To date, over 180 countries have ratified the convention.

Disability-inclusive development: Many organizations, including the World Bank, are working to ensure that development projects and programs are inclusive of people with disabilities. This includes providing access to education, healthcare, and employment opportunities.

Accessibility laws and regulations: Governments around the world are enacting laws and regulations to ensure that buildings, transportation, and information technology are accessible to people with disabilities. For example, the Americans with Disabilities Act (ADA) requires public places to provide reasonable accommodations for people with disabilities.

Disability rights advocacy: There are numerous disability rights organizations around the world that are advocating for the rights of people with disabilities. These organizations work to raise awareness, promote policy changes, and provide support and resources to people with disabilities.

Technology innovations: Advancements in technology have made it possible for people with disabilities to participate in society in ways that were previously impossible. For example, screen readers and text-to-speech software allow people with visual impairments to access digital content, while voice recognition technology enables people with mobility impairments to use computers and other devices.

How are people treated with disability during war times?

People with disabilities face unique challenges during wartime, as they may be at increased risk of injury or harm and may have difficulty accessing essential services and support. Here are some specific examples of how people with disabilities are treated during war times:

Displacement and refugee camps: People with disabilities who are displaced by war or become refugees often face significant barriers to accessing essential services such as healthcare, food, and shelter. Many refugee camps are not designed with the needs of people with disabilities in mind, which can make it difficult for them to navigate their surroundings and access necessary resources.

Use of explosive weapons: The use of explosive weapons in populated areas during armed conflict can result in high numbers of civilian casualties, including people with disabilities. Explosive weapons such as landmines, cluster bombs, and improvised explosive devices can cause permanent disabilities such as amputations, blindness, and traumatic brain injuries.

Lack of access to medical care: People with disabilities may have difficulty accessing medical care during war times due to damage to healthcare facilities or lack of resources. This can lead to untreated or poorly treated conditions, which can have long-term consequences.

Targeted violence: People with disabilities may be targeted for violence or abuse during armed conflict due to perceived vulnerabilities or as a result of discriminatory attitudes. For example, people with intellectual or psychosocial disabilities may be perceived as a threat or as less valuable, and may be subjected to violence or abuse.

Humanitarian aid: Humanitarian aid organizations may not have the resources or expertise to adequately address the needs of people with disabilities during war times. This can result in a lack of access to essential services and support, as well as a lack of inclusion in decision-making processes related to humanitarian response.

How are disabled people treated today?

People with disabilities face a range of experiences and treatment depending on the country, culture, and context. However, in general, there have been significant advancements in recent years towards promoting disability rights and creating more inclusive societies. Here are some specific examples of how people with disabilities are treated today:

Accessibility: Many countries have laws and regulations requiring public spaces and services to be accessible to people with disabilities. This includes building codes, transportation regulations, and web accessibility standards. There has also been a greater focus on making cultural events and entertainment more accessible through the use of assistive technology, sign language interpreters, and audio description.

Inclusive education: There has been a growing emphasis on inclusive education, which aims to provide all students with the support they need to succeed in mainstream classrooms. This includes providing assistive technology, specialized teaching methods, and accommodations such as extra time on tests.

Employment: There has been a push to increase employment opportunities for people with disabilities, including through anti-discrimination laws and affirmative action programs. Many companies are also recognizing the value of a diverse workforce and are actively seeking to hire people with disabilities.

Healthcare: There has been greater awareness of the healthcare needs of people with disabilities, and efforts are being made to ensure that healthcare providers are trained to provide appropriate care. This includes providing accessible facilities and equipment, providing communication aids such as sign language interpreters and easy-to-read materials, and ensuring that medical staff have a good understanding of the needs of people with disabilities.

Disability rights advocacy: There are many disability rights organizations around the world that are advocating for the rights of people with disabilities. These organizations work to raise awareness, promote policy changes, and provide support and resources to people with disabilities. They also work to combat negative stereotypes and discrimination.

Disability And Sports

There have been significant efforts in recent years to promote disability in sports and increase opportunities for people with disabilities to participate in athletics. Here are some specific examples of what is being done:

Paralympic Games: The Paralympic Games is a major international multi-sport event for athletes with disabilities. The games feature a wide range of sports, including athletics, swimming, wheelchair basketball, and sitting volleyball. The Paralympic Games help to raise awareness of disability sports and provide a platform for athletes to showcase their skills.

Adaptive sports programs: Many sports organizations have developed adaptive sports programs that provide opportunities for people with disabilities to participate in sports. These programs may include wheelchair basketball, adaptive skiing, and wheelchair racing. These programs help to provide accessible and inclusive sports opportunities for people with disabilities.

Inclusive sports facilities: There has been a push to make sports facilities more inclusive and accessible to people with disabilities. This includes providing wheelchair ramps, accessible seating, and specialized equipment such as hand-cycles and racing wheelchairs.

Disability sports associations: There are many disability sports associations around the world that are working to promote disability sports and provide support to athletes with disabilities. These associations may provide coaching, training, and resources to athletes with disabilities.

Media coverage: There has been a greater focus on media coverage of disability sports, which helps to raise awareness of the achievements of athletes with disabilities and promote greater acceptance of disability in sports. This includes coverage of major events such as the Paralympic Games, as well as local disability sports events.

Disabled Athletes

Here is a list of famous sports figures who are disabled:

Tanni Grey-Thompson - A retired British Paralympic wheelchair racer who won 16 Paralympic medals and set over 30 world records.

Jean Driscoll - A retired American wheelchair racer who won 12 Paralympic medals and 5 Boston Marathons.

Oscar Pistorius - A South African sprinter who competed in both the Paralympic and Olympic Games despite having a double amputation.

Ellie Simmonds - A British swimmer who has won 5 Paralympic gold medals and set multiple world records.

Casey Martin - An American professional golfer who has a degenerative circulatory disorder that affects his legs.

Aaron Fotheringham - An American wheelchair athlete who is known for inventing extreme wheelchair stunts and performing in the Nitro Circus Live Tour.

Rick Hansen - A Canadian wheelchair athlete who completed a 26-month wheelchair trip around the world to raise awareness for spinal cord injury research.

Natalia Partyka - A Polish table tennis player who was born without a right hand but has competed in both the Paralympic and Olympic Games.

Kurt Fearnley - An Australian wheelchair racer and Paralympic gold medalist who has competed in multiple marathons and ultra-marathons.

Tatyana McFadden - A Russian-born American wheelchair racer who has won 17 Paralympic medals and 24 world championship medals.

In The Eyes Of God

In the eyes of God, we are all the same,
No matter our ability, body, or name.
For God sees beyond the surface of our being,
And loves us all, regardless of what we're seeing.

Though the world may see disability as a flaw,
God sees each of us as a unique creation, raw.
God made us all with purpose and intention,
And sees the beauty in every dimension.

For God's love is not limited by our ability,
But embraces us in our full vulnerability.
God sees our struggles and our triumphs,
And celebrates with us in each of life's bumps.

And though the world may judge and dismiss,
God sees our true worth, and that we exist.
God loves us all, without any reservation,
And sees us all as part of God's grand creation.

So let us embrace and celebrate our diversity,
Knowing that we are all part of God's tapestry.
For God sees us all with love and admiration,
And cherishes each of us in the Creator's divine creation.

Flyboy

Once upon a time, in a world full of superheroes and villains, there lived a young African-American boy named Malik. Malik had always dreamed of becoming a superhero, but he was born with a disability that left him unable to walk. Despite this, Malik never let his disability define him, and he was determined to find a way to use his abilities to help others.

One day, while exploring an old abandoned laboratory, Malik stumbled upon a mysterious vial of glowing liquid. Without thinking, he drank the potion, hoping that it would somehow give him the strength he needed to become a superhero.

At first, nothing happened, and Malik began to worry that he had made a mistake. But then he felt a strange energy coursing through his body, and suddenly he was lifted off the ground and into the air. Malik had gained the power of flight, and he knew that he had become the hero he always dreamed of being.

As he flew through the city, Malik saw a group of bank robbers making their getaway in a stolen car. Without hesitation, he swooped down and picked up the car, lifting it high into the sky and bringing it to a stop. The robbers were caught, and Malik was hailed as a hero.

From that day on, Malik became known as "Flyboy," the superhero who could fly and lift anything with his incredible strength. He used his powers to help those in need, rescuing people from burning buildings and stopping criminals in their tracks.

But Malik never forgot where he came from, and he made it his mission to inspire other disabled children to believe in themselves and their abilities. He visited schools and hospitals, sharing his story and encouraging others to find their own inner strength.

And so, Malik became not just a superhero, but a symbol of hope and inspiration for all those who faced challenges in their lives. He proved that anyone can be a hero, no matter what their abilities may be, and he changed the world for the better, one flight at a time.

A Spirit Unbroken

He traveled the world with a heart full of wonder,
A spirit unbroken, though his legs were under,
A disability he had, but it did not define,
The world was his oyster, and he was to shine.

He saw the towering mountains of Peru,
The sparkling waters of the Caribbean blue,
He felt the heat of the African sun,
And danced with the locals, having fun.

He climbed the Great Wall in China with pride,
And rode a camel in the desert, side by side,
He explored ancient ruins in Greece,
And marveled at the art of the Italian masterpiece.

He faced challenges and obstacles along the way,
But he never let his disability lead him astray,
He found ways to adapt, to make it all work,
His spirit and determination, never to shirk.

He met people of all kinds, from every land,
And learned of their cultures, their way of life so grand,
He found beauty in their differences and in their unity,
A world full of diversity, and so much opportunity.

And so he traveled the world with a heart full of wonder,
A spirit unbroken, and legs that sometimes made him ponder,
But he knew that his disability was not a hindrance,
But rather a reminder of his strength and resilience.

Sophia

Once upon a time, in a small village in the mountains, there lived a young girl named Sophia. Sophia was born with a disability, and as a result, her parents feared for her future. They thought that her disability would hold her back from achieving anything great in life. But Sophia had a spirit that could not be broken, and a heart that was determined to help others.

Sophia grew up to be a remarkable young woman. She had a passion for helping people and a desire to see the world. Despite her physical limitations, Sophia refused to let her disability hold her back. She began to volunteer at a local shelter, where she helped care for the animals and provide comfort to those in need. Her love for helping others continued to grow, and she knew that she wanted to do more.

One day, Sophia stumbled upon a volunteer organization that provided aid and support to communities in need around the world. She knew that this was her calling, and she immediately signed up to become a volunteer. Sophia's first trip took her to a small village in Africa, where she worked alongside other volunteers to build a school for the local children. She also helped to provide food, medical care, and clean water to the village.

Sophia's experiences in Africa only fueled her desire to help others. Over the years, she traveled to many different countries, always with a smile on her face and a heart full of compassion. She helped to build homes, schools, and hospitals. She cared for the sick, the elderly, and the vulnerable. She fought for the rights of those who had been marginalized, and she never gave up on her mission to make the world a better place.

Despite the challenges she faced due to her disability, Sophia never once let it hold her back. In fact, it was her disability that gave her the strength and resilience to face any obstacle that came her way. Her unwavering determination and selflessness inspired everyone around her, and she became a beacon of hope to those who had lost faith in humanity.

As Sophia grew older, she knew that her time to travel the world and help others was coming to an end. But her legacy lived on through the countless lives she had touched and the many communities she had helped to build. Sophia had shown the world that disability was not a limitation, but rather a gift that could be used to make the world a better place.

In the end, Sophia passed away surrounded by the love of her family and the gratitude of those she had helped. But her spirit and her legacy lived on, inspiring others to follow in her footsteps and make a difference in the world. Sophia may have been disabled, but she was a hero in every sense of the word.

Tom Transformed

In a bustling city, there lived a man named Tom. Tom was known for his cruel and insensitive jokes about disabled people. He would laugh and poke fun at anyone who looked or acted different, never realizing the hurt and pain he caused.

One day, as Tom was rushing to a meeting, he stumbled and fell down a flight of stairs. He hit his head hard, and when he woke up, he found that he had lost the ability to walk. Tom was devastated, and his heart was filled with fear and despair. He felt the weight of his past actions, and he knew that he had been wrong to mock and ridicule those who were disabled.

As he lay in his hospital bed, Tom had a lot of time to think. He realized that he had been blind to the beauty and strength of disabled people, and he was filled with regret for his past behavior. He knew that he needed to make amends, to find a way to redeem himself and help others see the error of their ways.

Tom began to spend his days in rehabilitation, pushing himself to regain his strength and mobility. He also began to volunteer at a local disability center, where he met and spoke with people who had disabilities. He listened to their stories, learned about their struggles and triumphs, and slowly began to see the world through their eyes.

Over time, Tom's heart began to change. He found joy in helping others, in advocating for their rights and dignity. He became a strong voice in the community, speaking out against discrimination and stigma. He shared his story with others, hoping to inspire them to be more respectful and understanding of disabled people.

Through his work and his advocacy, Tom found a new sense of purpose and meaning. He realized that he had been given a second chance, a chance to make things right and to make a positive impact in the world. He became a champion for disability rights, working tirelessly to ensure that everyone, regardless of ability, was treated with kindness and respect.

In the end, Tom's accident had turned out to be a blessing in disguise. It had opened his eyes to the beauty and strength of the disabled community, and it had given him a chance to make a real difference in the world. Tom's journey had been long and difficult, but he had emerged from it a better, kinder, and more compassionate man.

What do you say 'disability' is?

1. A physical limitations and impairments.
2. Mental health conditions such as depression, anxiety or PTSD.
3. The need for accessibility in public spaces and transportation.
4. The challenges that disabled people face in their daily lives.
5. Famous individuals with disabilities, such as Stephen Hawking or Frida Kahlo.
6. The social stigma and discrimination against people with disabilities.
7. Special education programs and accommodations in schools.
8. Assistive technology, such as wheelchairs, hearing aids or prosthetic limbs.
9. The need for job opportunities and inclusion in the workforce for people with disabilities.
10. Disability rights activism and advocacy groups.

What can 'disability' be?

When people hear the word "disability," positive thoughts and associations can also come to mind. Here are some examples:

The strength, resilience, and determination of disabled people to overcome their challenges and achieve their goals.

The unique perspectives and abilities that disabled people bring to the world.

The diverse and vibrant disability culture that celebrates disabled identity and pride.

The inclusive and accessible practices that enable disabled people to participate fully in society.

The supportive and caring communities that exist to empower and uplift disabled individuals.

The advancements in assistive technology and medical treatments that have improved the lives of disabled people.

The social and political progress that has been made towards recognizing and protecting disability rights and equality.

The inspiring stories of disabled individuals who have accomplished great things in their lives, such as athletes, artists, entrepreneurs, and activists.

The potential for disability to foster empathy, compassion, and understanding in others.

The opportunities for innovation and creativity that arise from the challenges of disability.

In recent years, there has been a growing awareness and recognition of the rights and needs of people with disabilities. This has led to improvements in areas such as accessibility, inclusion, and employment opportunities. Technology has also played a significant role in enhancing the quality of life for people with disabilities, with advances such as assistive devices, communication tools, and adaptive software.

Looking ahead, it is possible that these trends will continue to evolve and expand. Governments, organizations, and individuals may continue to work towards creating more accessible and inclusive environments, policies, and practices. This could lead to greater social and economic participation for people with disabilities, as well as improved health and well-being outcomes.

At the same time, there may also be challenges and obstacles to overcome. These could include issues such as discrimination, stigma, and lack of resources or support. Climate change, pandemics, and other global crises could also have an impact on the lives of people with disabilities, particularly those who are already marginalized or vulnerable.

Ultimately, the future for people with disabilities will depend on a variety of factors, including societal attitudes, policy decisions, technological developments, and individual actions. It is important for all of us to continue working towards a more equitable and inclusive future for everyone, regardless of ability.

A Mother's Love

Once upon a time, there was a mother who had a child with a disability. Despite the challenges that came with raising a child with special needs, the mother loved her child deeply and fiercely.

One day, the child asked the mother a difficult question: "Do you ever wish that I was never born?" The mother's heart broke at the thought of her child feeling unloved or unwanted.

Without hesitation, the mother wrapped her arms around her child and said, "Never! I could never wish that you were never born. You are the light of my life, the joy in my heart, and I love you more than words could ever express."

The child's face lit up with a smile, and tears filled the mother's eyes as she held her child close. In that moment, the mother knew that her love for her child was unconditional and unwavering, no matter what challenges they may face.

As the child grew up, they faced many obstacles and setbacks, but the mother was always there to support and encourage them. Together, they navigated the ups and downs of life with love, patience, and resilience.

Years later, the child became an adult, and the mother watched with pride as they pursued their dreams and achieved their goals. Though there were still challenges to overcome, the mother and child faced them together, knowing that their love was stronger than any obstacle.

And as the mother looked back on their journey together, she knew without a doubt that she had never regretted a single moment of her child's life. For in her child, she had found the greatest gift of all: love.